WOMEN OVER
40
ARE BETTER BECAUSE...

Written by
Herbert I. Kavet
and
Jill A. Szynski

Illustrated by
Martin Riskin

Manufactured in the United States of America

30 29 28 27 26 25 24 23 22 21 20 19 18 17 16 15 14 13 12 11 10 9 8 7 6 5 4 3 2

Ivory Tower Publishing Co., Inc.
125 Walnut St., P.O. Box 9132, Watertown, MA 02272-9132
Telephone #: (617) 923-1111   Fax #: (617) 923-8839

WOMEN OVER **40** ARE BETTER BECAUSE...

They start to make some real contributions in their field.

WOMEN OVER 40 ARE BETTER BECAUSE...

They have a handle on all the latest fashions.

WOMEN OVER 40 ARE BETTER BECAUSE...

They know how to start a car on fiercely cold mornings.

WOMEN OVER 40 ARE BETTER BECAUSE...

The kids are finally out of the house.

WOMEN OVER **40** ARE BETTER BECAUSE...

They start to hang around with new grandparents.
Of course, most are much older than they are.

WOMEN OVER 40 ARE BETTER BECAUSE...

They don't expect as much foreplay because
they want to get to the heart of the matter.

WOMEN OVER **40** ARE BETTER BECAUSE...

They actually look forward to dull evenings at home.

WOMEN OVER 40 ARE BETTER BECAUSE...

They start taking a serious interest in investment and savings plans.

WOMEN OVER 40 ARE BETTER BECAUSE...

They will let you watch football, basketball or any sport
on TV and not be upset because you're ignoring them.

They can shop for a car with the acuteness of an automotive engineer.

WOMEN OVER 40 ARE BETTER BECAUSE...

They will respect you in the morning.

WOMEN OVER 40 ARE BETTER BECAUSE...

They can eat a double-fudge chocolate sundae and not get any pimples, but they have to go to 3 aerobic classes to work it off—so they skip it anyway.

WOMEN OVER 40 ARE BETTER BECAUSE...

They can smoothly put down propositions from the drunkest chauvinist.

They've tried every diet known to womankind, but no longer throw out their oversized clothes at the end of a successful one.

WOMEN OVER 40 ARE BETTER BECAUSE...

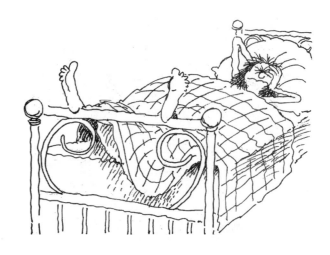

They know when they've had enough to drink and nothing
is worth that hangover the next day.

WOMEN OVER 40 ARE BETTER BECAUSE...

They have achieved a reasonable accommodation
with their exercise program.

WOMEN OVER 40 ARE BETTER BECAUSE...

They have great lingerie collections.

They can usually find a "contact" to help them out with difficult situations.

WOMEN
OVER
40
ARE BETTER
BECAUSE...

They have kids to help out with the real tough jobs.

WOMEN OVER 40 ARE BETTER BECAUSE...

They don't contemplate suicide at the end of an affair.

WOMEN OVER 40 ARE BETTER BECAUSE...

They are no longer very concerned about being "with it".

WOMEN OVER 40 ARE BETTER BECAUSE...

They have learned to live with pets.

WOMEN
OVER
40
ARE BETTER
BECAUSE...

They can't be pressured into driving faster than they feel comfortable doing.

WOMEN OVER 40 ARE BETTER BECAUSE...

Fine establishments actually solicit them to carry their credit cards.

WOMEN OVER 40 ARE BETTER BECAUSE...

They know how to handle temporary lapses in performance.

WOMEN OVER 40 ARE BETTER BECAUSE...

Banks start to trust them.

WOMEN OVER 40 ARE BETTER BECAUSE...

They are wise enough to enjoy sports as a spectator rather than risk injuring themselves.

They realize their father was right when he said it was as easy
to fall in love with a rich guy as a poor one.

WOMEN OVER 40 ARE BETTER BECAUSE...

They start dressing for comfort rather than blindly
following the latest styles.

They finally realize that their mother isn't the greatest cook in the world.
At least she remembers that you hate cauliflower.

WOMEN OVER **40** ARE BETTER BECAUSE...

They can finally afford all the things they no longer want.

WOMEN OVER 40 ARE BETTER BECAUSE...

They don't believe all the things men whisper in their ear.
They don't get terribly embarrassed by them either.

WOMEN OVER 40 ARE BETTER BECAUSE...

They are happy to hang out on the couch on Friday nights instead of going out.

WOMEN OVER **40** ARE BETTER BECAUSE...

They can see just fine if they squint a little during candlelight dinners.

WOMEN OVER 40 ARE BETTER BECAUSE...

They know how to organize a truly great party.

WOMEN OVER 40 ARE BETTER BECAUSE...

They are smart enough to hire someone to do the cleaning.

WOMEN OVER 40 ARE BETTER BECAUSE...

They won't blush if you take them to an X-rated movie.

WOMEN OVER 40 ARE BETTER BECAUSE...

They are occasionally offered assistance from totally unexpected sources.

WOMEN
OVER
40

ARE BETTER
BECAUSE...

They replace the "Save The Whales" bumper sticker with
"World's Greatest Mom".

They may have trouble with forgetting things but they have their reminder systems down pat.

WOMEN OVER **40**
ARE BETTER BECAUSE...

They know being alone is better than being with someone they don't like.

WOMEN OVER 40 ARE BETTER BECAUSE...

They know their exact alcohol limits.

WOMEN OVER 40 ARE BETTER BECAUSE...

They can remember the punch line to at least 3 dirty jokes.

WOMEN OVER 40 ARE BETTER BECAUSE...

They will be amused if you take them parking.

WOMEN OVER 40 ARE BETTER BECAUSE...

They fantasize about going into business for themselves.

They don't care where their husbands go when they go out
as long as they don't have to go with them.

WOMEN OVER 40 ARE BETTER BECAUSE...

They don't nag–they gently remind you.

WOMEN OVER 40 ARE BETTER BECAUSE...

They find obscene phone calls a mildly amusing form of entertainment.

WOMEN OVER 40 ARE BETTER BECAUSE...

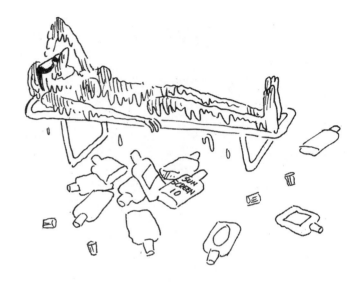

They can single-handedly support the entire sunscreen industry.

They have more womanly figures.

WOMEN OVER 40 ARE BETTER BECAUSE...

Their eyes are as good as ever; it's just that their arms are growing shorter.

WOMEN OVER 40 ARE BETTER BECAUSE...

They find themselves on virtually every junk mail list in the country.
During the Christmas season they receive 43 full color catalogs every day.

WOMEN OVER **40** ARE BETTER BECAUSE...

They have great liquor cabinets.

WOMEN OVER 40 ARE BETTER BECAUSE...

They can go to the movies alone on a Saturday night
and not feel the least embarrassed.

WOMEN OVER 40 ARE BETTER BECAUSE...

They live in a place where noisy parties, littering, sex fiends, drug dealers and people crossing against the lights are all frowned upon.

WOMEN OVER 40 ARE BETTER BECAUSE...

They don't fall to pieces if you see them without their makeup.

WOMEN OVER 40 ARE BETTER BECAUSE...

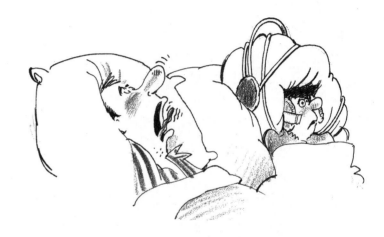

They can tune out even the worst snoring.

They don't believe all the ads for moisturizers and skin restorers,
but they buy them anyway.

WOMEN OVER 40 ARE BETTER BECAUSE...

They know exactly what they like, and what they like costs a fortune.

They don't care if their man has a night out with the boys
while they stay home and sleep.

WOMEN OVER 40 ARE BETTER BECAUSE...

Expletives don't embarrass them and they are able to use them at appropriate moments.

WOMEN OVER 40 ARE BETTER BECAUSE...

They no longer sleep soundly through the night
but can fall asleep instantly at any dull meeting.

WOMEN OVER 40 ARE BETTER BECAUSE...

They finally realize that no one cares anymore about what they did in high school.

WOMEN OVER 40 ARE BETTER BECAUSE...

They are not afraid to redecorate.

WOMEN OVER 40 ARE BETTER BECAUSE...

They are not afraid to include a few weirdos among their friends.

They have a favorite mechanic who is happy to help them out in an emergency.

WOMEN OVER 40 ARE BETTER BECAUSE...

Their years of expertise enable them to know exactly what is going wrong with their cars. Still, they can't get anyone competent to fix it.

WOMEN OVER 40 ARE BETTER BECAUSE...

They appreciate the advantages of control-top pantyhose.

WOMEN OVER 40 ARE BETTER BECAUSE...

They know the proper pronunciation of at least three wines that they like and don't give a hoot about which goes well with what foods.

They don't pretend to be virgins.

WOMEN OVER **40** ARE BETTER BECAUSE...

They are willing to leave boring parties early.

They've stopped smoking, drink with moderation and eat sensibly. Still, they always carry antacid pills.

WOMEN OVER 40 ARE BETTER BECAUSE...

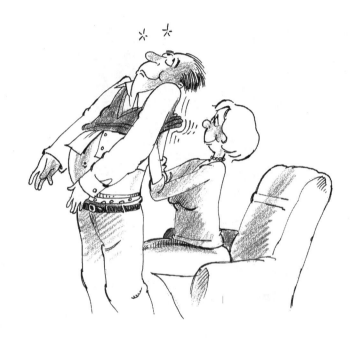

They know just what it takes to make their man feel good.

They finally stopped waiting for the baby fat to disappear.

WOMEN OVER 40 ARE BETTER BECAUSE...

They can afford an occasional splurge.

WOMEN OVER 40 ARE BETTER BECAUSE...

They can buy a car without soliciting advice from their father.

WOMEN OVER 40 ARE BETTER BECAUSE...

They can recognize and pronounce the names of at least 3 French wines.

They can offer a critical analysis of every fad diet
to come along in the last 20 years.

WOMEN OVER 40 ARE BETTER BECAUSE...

They know exactly which foods are incompatible with their digestive systems.

They won't make you sleep in the middle of their stuffed animal collection.

WOMEN OVER 40 ARE BETTER BECAUSE...

Men at the office actually solicit their advice.

WOMEN OVER 40 ARE BETTER BECAUSE...

They don't catch colds very often but hurt for a week
after moving the refrigerator.

WOMEN OVER 40

ARE BETTER BECAUSE...

They realize that no matter how many sit-ups and leg raises they do, they cannot recapture their 17-year-old figures.

They have a few favorite secret recipes that can get them through any crisis.

WOMEN OVER 40 ARE BETTER BECAUSE...

They truly know the value of a good friend.

WOMEN OVER 40 ARE BETTER BECAUSE...

They can find something attractive in any 21-year-old guy.

WOMEN OVER 40 ARE BETTER BECAUSE...

They are never too scared to enjoy sex.

WOMEN OVER 40 ARE BETTER BECAUSE...

They no longer apologize for gay or weird friends.

WOMEN
OVER
40
ARE BETTER
BECAUSE...

Their bookshelf is overflowing with "How To" and "Self Improvement" books that they don't bother to read.

WOMEN OVER 40 ARE BETTER BECAUSE...

You no longer have to give them birthday presents. They plot revenge on people who give them books like this one.

You may send directly to us for the books below. Postage is $1.50 for the first book and $0.50 for each additional book.

TRADE PAPERBACK BOOKS $5.95

2400	Sex On Your Birthday
2402	Confessions From Bathroom
2403	Good Bonking Guide
2404	Sex Slave
2405	Mid-Life Sex
2406	World's Sex Records
2407	40 Happens
2408	30: The Big Three-Oh
2409	50 Happens
2411	Geriatric Sex Guide
2412	Golf Shots
2415	Birthdays Happen
2416	Absolutely Worst Fart
2417	Women Over 30 Are Better
2418	9 Months in Sac
2419	Cucumbers Are Better
2421	Honeymoon Guide
2422	Eat Yourself Healthy
2423	Sex After 40?
2424	Sex After 50?
2425	Women Over 40 Are Better
2426	Women Over 50 Are Better
2427	Over The Hill
2428	Beer Is Better
2429	Married to a Computer
2430	Sex After 30?
2431	Happy B'day Old Fart
2432	Big Weenies
2433	Games Play With Pussy
2434	Sex And Marriage
2435	Baby's First Year
2436	How To Love A New Yorker
2437	The Retirement Book
2438	Dog Farts
2439	Handling His Mid-Life Crisis
2440	How To Love A Texan
2441	Bedtime Stories...Kitty
2442	Bedtime Stories...Doggie
2443	60 With Sizzle!
2444	The Wedding Night
2445	Woman's Birthday Wish
2446	The PMS Book
2447	The Pregnant Father
2448	Games Play In Bed
2449	The Barf Book
2450	How To Pick Up Girls
2451	How To Pick Up Guys
2452	Driving Amongst Idiots
2453	Beginner's Sex Manual
2454	Get Well
2455	Unspeakably Rotten Cartoons
2456	For A Million Bucks...
2457	Hooters
2458	Adult Connect the Dots
2459	Once Upon A Mattress
2460	Golfing Amongst Idiots
2461	Marry Me, Marry Me
2462	Smokers Are People, Too

FUN BOOKS $3.00

2026	Games Play In Bed
2034	You're Over 40 When...
2042	Cucumbers Are Better
2064	Wedding Night
2067	It's Time To Retire When...
2068	Sex Manual...Over 30
2102	You're Over 50 When...
2127	Your Golf Game
2131	The Fart Book
2136	The Shit List
2148	Dear Teacher
2166	Survived Catholic School
2177	You're Over The Hill
2180	Italian Sex Manual
2181	Jewish Sex Manual
2192	You're Over 30 When...
2195	Beer Is Better
2203	The Last Fart Book
2205	Sex After 40?
2210	Sex After Marriage?
2213	Women Over 50 Are Better
2217	Sex After 50?
2224	Life's A Picnic...Big Weenie
2225	Women Over 40 Are Better
2226	C.R.S.
2227	Happy Birthday/Year Older
2229	You're A Redneck
2233	Small Busted Women
2234	You're Over 60
2235	You Know You're Over 70
2236	Nose Picker's Guide
2237	55 & Picking Up Speed
2240	Dumb Men Jokes
2241	Cats Are Better Than Men
2242	Working Woman's Doodle
2243	Working Man's Doodle
2244	Words of Wisdom
2245	Potty Potpourri

HARDCOVER BOOKS $8.95

2350	Sailing
2351	Computers
2352	Cats
2353	Tennis
2354	Bowling
2355	Parenting
2356	Fitness
2357	Golf
2358	Fishing
2359	Bathrooms
2360	Biking
2361	Running
2362	Skiing
2363	Doctors
2364	Lawyers
2365	Teachers
2366	Nurses
2367	Firefighters
2368	Marines

Ivory Tower Publishing Co., Inc., 125 Walnut St., P.O. Box 9132, Watertown, MA 02272-9132   Tel: (617) 923-1111